Just Like You

CRYSTAL JORDAN

ILLUSTRATED BY JANAKA THILAKARATHNE

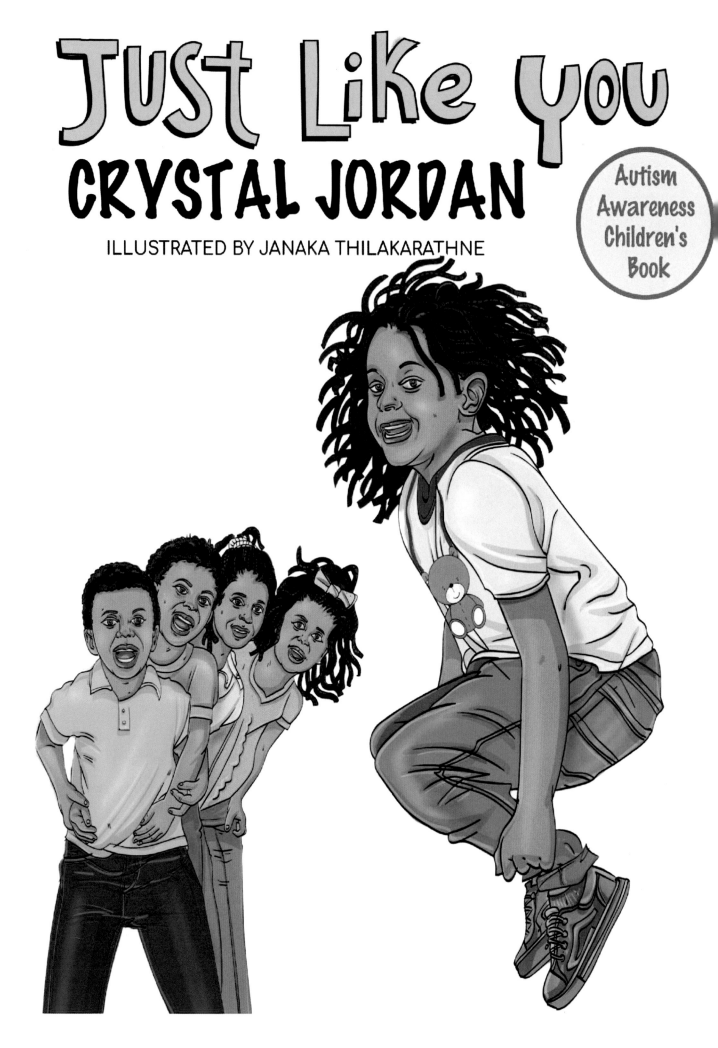

Do you want to feature "Just Like You"?
Don't hesitate to get in touch with Crystal by e-mail at
press@zachariahworld.com

Are you interested in becoming a published author?
Get in touch with us today
sistahoodpublishing.com/bookme
heysis@sistahoodpublishing.com

Just Like You
By: Crystal Jordan
Illustration By: Janaka Thilakarathne
Published by Crystal Jordan
www.zachariahworld.com

ISBN: 978-1-7364529-1-2

Just Like You

By: **Crystal Jordan**

BLACK KID WITH AUTISM!

LIVING IN A BIG WORLD!

ALL CHILDREN ARE NORMAL!

HOWEVER, ZACH HAS HIDDEN SUPERPOWERS!

ONLY CERTAIN PEOPLE IN THE WORLD WOULD

UNDERSTAND.

HE IS ATYPICAL!

BUT HE IS JUST LIKE YOU AND ME.

HE IS LEARNING AND GROWING EVERY DAY.

JUST IN A DIFFERENT WAY!

Preface

As the mother of a child living with ASD (Autism Spectrum Disorder), I was devastated by the news but knew I had to be my son's advocate. My son is non-verbal, and it has become a mission for me to educate more people, especially in the black and brown communities, about Autism. I passionately believe that people must be introduced to this topic, and more awareness should be rendered to their children to help educate them.

Just like you were designed for parents to read aloud to their children and introduce Autism Spectrum Disorder to them. I believe ignorance is not bliss if one takes the time to learn something new. Perhaps this book will shed more light on the autistic community and help educate those living with it.

Dear Zachariah,

My dear son, someday, I hope that you will be proud of me for creating this book for kids just like you. I look forward to educating and introducing Autism Spectrum Disorder to the black community and the world. You have opened my eyes to see the world differently. I am very grateful for the patience you have taught me and the true meaning of unconditional love. You are my favorite person of all time, and no one on the planet can take your place in my heart. Mommy loves you and can't wait to share and raise awareness about Autism and help the world embrace it.

Love, Mom

Zachariah was a joyful baby boy from birth. He was the pure definition of a beautiful black baby, with very curly hair and lovely melanin skin. He also had a bright smile that would light up your day, even if all wasn't going well.

Zachariah was diagnosed at the age of two with Autism. He is non-verbal, unable to speak or form words like other children his age.

His parents were very shocked by the doctor's diagnosis of their son. His mom, Ms. Jordan was mostly sad, but she always prayed and believed that Zachariah would turn out to be an amazing boy.

Despite her son's diagnosis, she knew he was special and is committed to always showing Zachariah how much he was loved.

He always had a way of bringing happiness and life into his room. He wasn't a boy of many words, but that did not stop him from expressing himself through art. He was full of life and joy. You may ask, "why didn't he talk much"?

The little boy mostly communicated using non-verbal cues and pointing gestures. For example, when he was happy, he would jump up and down. He would clap his hands and tap his fingers, or when sad, he would have a meltdown.

Ms. Jordan worked hard for months to get Zachariah into school. Well, the day had finally come, and Zachariah's first day has arrived.

Ms. Jordan was incredibly excited for her little boy to mingle and make new play buddies. At the same time, however, she was scared that some kids would not understand her baby boy and might make fun of him.

"And who do we have here?" asked an excited Mrs. Patience, the Kindergarten teacher.

Mrs. Patience was going to be Zachariah's class teacher. The boy instantly liked his new teacher and went straight to hug her.

He kept pointing at her glasses and looking back at his parents. "Oh, haha! Don't worry, Mrs. Patience! I think Zachariah is trying to say he really likes your glasses," explained Ms. Jordan.

"It's okay, I read his IEP report, and I am aware that he is on the spectrum. Zachariah is in good hands, and he will have speech therapy twice a week."

Zachariah went to a seat in the corner away from the other children while Mrs. Patience began talking to Ms. Jordan about her concerns for the school year.

"Zachariah was diagnosed with non-verbal Autism at two years old. He can barely say any words. His speech isn't as developed as it should be," said Ms. Jordan.

She tried to keep herself from crying, but Mrs. Patience places her hand on her shoulder to calm her down.

"I know what you are going through. I have a nephew just like him. The boy is such a delight to the family, and Zachariah looks like a joyful baby boy, too!"

"I took some time to look over his IEP report, and we are going to start working on his goals today. Don't worry, Ms. Jordan, Zachariah is in good hands."

"I love the fact that this has never stopped him from being a happy kid. I feel much better knowing that you have taken the time to go over his report, and it shows me that you will take care of my boy," replied Ms. Jordan.

"Ah, ha-ha! Is this for me, Zachariah? Why, thank you, little angel. This is beautiful! Did you draw it?" asked an impressed Mrs. Patience.

Zachariah nodded with a big smile on his face. He brought with him a pretty drawing of a lily for his class teacher. The boy may not have been a chatterbox, but he was loud when it came to art.

Holding back tears of joy , his parents waved goodbye. They were just so happy to see their boy excited about learning. Mrs. Patience took hold of Zachariah's hand and walked into the classroom.

"Good morning, class! I have a new friend for you. Say hi to Zachariah!"

"Good morning, Mrs. Patience! Hello Zachariah, welcome to our class. It is fun to be here, and we hope you enjoy!" replied the little boys and girls in unison.

Zachariah just looked around and grabbed his teacher's leg.

"Zachariah is non-verbal and on the spectrum.
He has very few words."
"Don't be shy, Zachariah!
We are nice people!" shouted Jax, his new deskmate.

The class started by introducing themselves to their new classmate. It was now Zachariah's turn, and he was extremely nervous. He started stimming and jumping up and down.

It was playtime and the kids began to play with each other, but Zachariah went to the corner to play with his toys alone. See, Zachariah does not play with other kids. Sometimes he plays next to the kids, but does not interact with them!

Jax walked up to Zachariah and introduced himself,
"Hey, my name is Jax."
He sat next to Zachariah, who continued playing with his
blocks. Jax helped Zachariah stack the blocks so tall that
they fell. Both boys laughed so much.
Liam came over to help them clean up since Mrs. Patience
said that playtime was almost done.

All kids began to clean up and Mrs. Patience played some music. Zachariah loved music and he started to dance.

He closed his eyes and danced to the beat of the song. The other students were so amazed that they started shouting and clapping.

Jax and Liam, who were good friends, talked about how they will make Zachariah their new best friend. They thought he was so cool.

"I think Zachariah is cool!" shouted a classmate.
"You go, Zachariah, you are so cool!" shouted Jax.

Mrs. Patience was completely shocked that Zachariah was
doing so well on his first day... she was impressed!
He may not use many words but he is indeed special.

All the kids surrounded Zachariah , hugged him, and gave him high fives. And just like that, he became the most popular boy in class.

Mrs. Patience said, "Class, it is time to sit." A phrase that Zachariah was used to hearing since he had joined ABA therapy.
Zachariah quickly went to sit at his assigned seat.

As the class returned to their seats, everyone was already on their feet, clapping and chanting, "Zachariah is the coolest. Forget about the rest."

At 10 am, the break bell rang. Jax and Liam walked to Zachariah and offered to show him around the school. They were very friendly and patient with him, and instantly became his friends.

Zachariah smiled, clapped his hands, and using his hands; he made a love heart sign. It was his way of saying thank you and that he also loved his classmates. They all went to play at the swings together.

Although Mrs. Patience kept a close eye on Zachariah, Jax and Liam took good care of their new friend. Zachariah was smiling , laughing, and playing aside with the other kids. It was indeed a great first day at school.

See, Zachariah is just like you!
But he is just atypical!

What is Autism?

Autism, or autism spectrum disorder (ASD), refers to a broad range of conditions characterized by challenges with social skills, repetitive behaviors, speech, and nonverbal communication. Today, there are 1 in 54 children in the United States who have autism, according to the Centers for Disease Control.

According to Autism Speaks, people with Autism are different, they have their own strengths and challenges. There are people with ASD who require significant support in their daily lives, and there are others who are more independent. There are a variety of ways in which they learn to think and solve problems, ranging from highly skilled to severely challenged.

A number of factors can influence the development of autism, and it's often associated with sensory sensitivities and medical disorders such as gastrointestinal (GI) or sleep disorders, as well as mental health problems such as anxiety, depression, and attention issues. (Autism Speaks)

Some developmental delays associated with autism can occur as early as age 2, and the disorder can be diagnosed by 18 months. Research has shown that early intervention leads to better outcomes in adulthood for individuals with autism. (Autism Speaks)

According to the CDC, minority groups tend to be diagnosed later and less often.

Fun Fact!
Boys are up to four times more likely to be diagnosed with Autism Spectrum Disorder than girls!

Signs and Symptoms

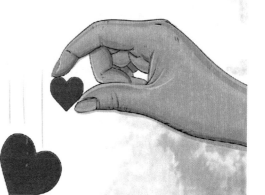

It is common for people with autism spectrum disorder to have social, emotional, and communication difficulties. Their daily activities might not change and they might repeat certain behaviors. Many autistic people also have different ways of learning, paying attention, or reacting to things. Signs of autism typically appear in early childhood and persist throughout a person's lifetime. You can find more information at (www.cdc.gov/ncbddd/autism/facts.html).

Children with ASD might:

· Not point at objects to show interest (for example, not point at an airplane flying over).

· Not look at objects when another person points at them.

· Have trouble relating to others or not have an interest in other people at all.

· Avoid eye contact and want to be alone.

· Have trouble understanding other people's feelings or talking about their feelings.

· Prefer not to be held or cuddled or might cuddle only when they want to.

· Appear to be unaware when people talk to them but respond to other sounds.

· Be very interested in people but not know how to talk, play, or relate to them.

· Repeat or echo words or phrases said to them or repeat words or phrases in place of normal language.

· Have trouble expressing their needs using typical words or motions.

· Repeat actions over and over again.

· Have trouble adapting when a routine changes.

· Have unusual reactions to the way things smell, taste, look, feel, or sound.

· Lose skills they once had (for example, stop saying words they were using).

· Please visit www.cdc.gov/ncbddd/autism/facts.html for more information.

Just Like You Word Glossary

Atypical - not typical; not conforming to the type; irregular; abnormal: atypical behavior.

Applied Behavior Analysis (ABA) - The science in which strategies derived from the principles of behavior are applied to improve socially significant behavior. ABA techniques are often used with children with autism to improve communication skills, play skills, social skills, academic skills, and self-care skills.

Non-vocal- individuals who don't use words. or speech; however, communication skills are present in another way usually through pointing, leading, or other actions such as picture exchange or sign language etc...

Non-verbal - Inability to use speech or words, other communication skills are also not present. Individuals often communicate by pointing, leading, or through their actions.

Nonverbal autism is a subset of autism where the person is unable to speak. It is estimated that 25% to 50% of children diagnosed with autism spectrum disorder (ASD) never develop spoken language beyond a few words or utterances.

Meltdown - An intense response to overwhelming circumstances a loss of behavioral control. Individuals with autism often have difficulty expressing themselves when they are feeling overwhelmed, which can lead to an involuntary coping mechanism a meltdown.

Self-stimulatory behavior (Stimming) - Repetitive body movements (such as rocking back and forth, hand flapping, clapping, vocal echoes, etc.) and/or repetitive movement of objects (such as spinning objects, lining up objects, etc.). Individuals with autism commonly engage in self-stimulatory behavior as a coping strategy for overstimulation.

Just Like You Word Glossary

504 Plan – It is a plan which ensures that a student with any sort of disability (physical or mental) must receive accommodations that will help him (or her) to achieve the deserved academic
success.

Individualized Education Plan (IEP) – IEP is designed to help kids succeed in school. It describes the goals set by the
school management for any child during his/her school
year, as well as any special support, needed to help achieve those goals.

What is an Individualized Education Plan (IEP)?
Formally speaking, an IEP is a legal document that contains the details of the personalized learning needs (and goals) for a child with any disability as defined by law, when the child attends a K-12 grade educational institution that receives public funding.

Scan Code

You can get freebies by visiting
zachariahworld.com/freebies

Scan Code

For resources, please visit
zachariahworld.com/resources

Collect All Our Books

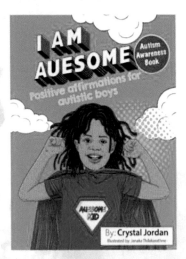

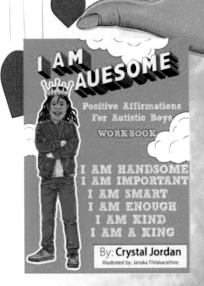

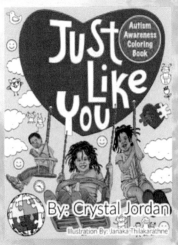

ZACHARIAH'S WORLD

ZACHARIAH'S WORLD

About the Author

Crystal Jordan was born and raised in Atlanta, Ga, where she attended Bauder College studying apparel design. She wrote this book to educate people in her community and the world. Her son was diagnosed at 2 years old with Autism Spectrum Disorder. She is sharing a piece of their life to help others who are afraid or ashamed to talk about theirs. She is an advocate for awareness about Autism and wants to keep being a voice. She is the owner of Amor Allure, an e-commerce women's boutique. Crystal created a brand centered around her son's disorder called "Zachariah's World," where children with Autism Spectrum Disorder are not forgotten but embraced.

"I am just a mom on a mission"- Crystal Jordan

Why did Crystal write this book?
Crystal made this book as a conversation starter for more people to become aware of Autism Spectrum Disorder. Moreover, she created this book to have more diversity in the market. Her son and many kids who are on the spectrum will see themselves in a book. She wants families to welcome this book into their homes and have an open discussion about Autism. Crystal wants the voices of children with this disorder to be heard but especially the children within the black community.

They are just like you, but they just have hidden superpowers.
– Crystal Jordan.

Scan Code

Stay updated this series at
www.zachariahworld.com

Made in the USA
Las Vegas, NV
22 January 2023

66050745R20021